Wallpapering
Step-by-Step

by Marian Lee Klenk

INTRODUCTION

A good quality wallpaper and a few basic skills are all you need to give one room or a whole house a fresh new look. Wallpapering offers one of the easiest, and relatively inexpensive, ways to redecorate. Wallpaper can provide a room with a subtle accent to set off a particular piece of furniture or woodwork; or it can be the color and design focus of the whole room. Many types of wallcoverings are available today from vinyl and vinyl-coated wallpapers to foils, flocked paper, grass cloth, and burlap, as well as more exotic murals, woodbark, and fabric wallcoverings.

This bulletin covers the basic steps, tools, and techniques needed to hang the most common types of wallpaper: basic vinyl or vinyl-coated paper. Other types of wallcoverings can be costly and should be hung by a professional. If you are a beginner, keep it simple and inexpensive.

CHAPTER I
HISTORY AND CURRENT USES OF WALLPAPER

Many historians believe wallpaper was first made and used in China, and indeed many of the earliest designs were Chinese scenes. The earliest wallpaper was hand painted and came in different-sized sheets of paper instead of rolls.

The Arabs obtained wallpaper in trade with the Orient and spread its use to the Middle East. Wallpaper eventually worked its way to Europe where it was first used in place of expensive tapestries. The earliest papers used in Europe were hand-painted floral and nature motifs imported from China.

The printing of paper by blocks was first introduced in Spain and Holland during the middle of the 16th century. Again, the paper was made in sheets of various sizes. In the 18th century, the present method of making long rolls of paper was adopted. As a result, wallpaper was no longer used only by royalty and the very elite, but was available to a broader group of people. However, the paper was still expensive, and could only be purchased by the wealthy.

With the coming of the industrial age in the 19th century and the mass production of machine-printed paper, people of more modest means could afford to buy wallpaper. By the middle of the 20th century, high-speed, low-cost production techniques coupled with new materials such as fabrics, plastic laminates and vinyls, and natural materials like cork and grass cloth, brought the greatest variety of wallcovering at a reasonable cost to the average consumer.

Today, wallpaper is used to enhance homes and to express individual tastes. Wallpaper is a master of disguise. It can change the apparent proportions of a room by visually enlarging or minimizing size. Wallpaper can give a sense of style, brighten a dark, gloomy room, or tone down and bring warmth to a large airy space.

Before you choose a paper, you must first know your own preferences and then figure out how to fit this preference into the needs of the interior of a particular room. Take into account the architectural features of the room (layout, size, and lighting).

In general, light, space, and continuity of the room will determine the color, pattern, and texture of the paper. While you may love small print designs, if you are papering a large room with a nine-foot ceiling, a small print will get lost, look too busy, and not achieve the effect that drew you to the design in the first place. Your favorite color may be overwhelming in a solid-color wallpaper. Find ways to incorporate the color in a complementary print which would bring out the tones of the woodwork or furniture. See what works best in the room and the home, and work with those design ideas along with your personal preferences in choosing your paper.

The focal point will also determine what paper design you choose. The focal point of a room is generally the first wall you see upon entering. However, it can be the wall that contains a decorative architectural feature such as a fireplace or handsome bay window.

Color can emphasize or diminish architectural features, or provide a warm or cool feeling to a room. Cool colors have green or blue undertones; warm colors have red or yellow undertones. Woodwork can be painted the background color of the paper to blend in, or an accent color in the paper to stand out. The colors in a paper may pick up the colors in a favorite rug or provide a warm textured look on the walls with the rug being the main accent in the room.

DECOR RULES OF THUMB

- The larger the room (height and wall space) the bigger the print design.
- Dark colors make a room seem smaller and warmer.
- Stripes make a room seem higher and larger.
- Geometric prints give a greater impression of space.
- Miniprints create a sense of space in a small room.
- Consider the architectural features of your home.
- Large prints cover imperfections in the walls better than small prints.
- Consider continuity. If a hallway opens onto your living room, the papers in each room should complement, not clash, with one another.
- Textured paper gives heaviness and warmth to a room.

Types of Paper

The various types of wallpaper available for purchase range from the machine-printed prepasted vinyl to the hand-printed reproduction antique designs. If you are a novice, it is best to learn on an inexpensive, machine-made, pretrimmed, prepasted vinyl. These papers are easy to apply and will endure more handling than other types of paper.

Applications

Most standard wallpaper contains many labor-saving application features. Other paper requires more time and patience. The following represent the most common types of paper applications.

Prepasted Wallpaper which has been coated with a water soluble adhesive. All you need to do is wet the paper to hang it.

Unpasted Paste is applied to the back of the paper with a brush. The type of paper determines what kind of paste you will need.

Scrubbable Vinyl and vinyl-coated papers can be washed with a mild soap. Vinyl papers are usually backed with paper or cloth. Vinyl-coated paper is simply coated with plastic and therefore less resistant to wear and tear. Both, however, are scrubbable to various degrees. Check out a sample piece to test the paper's durability when scrubbing.

Pretrimmed/Untrimmed Almost all paper comes in pretrimmed rolls. The selvage (a blank strip along the edge of the paper) has been trimmed at the factory.

Reinforced Backed/Strippable Many wallpapers (particularly the vinyl-backed papers) are strippable. You can remove the wallpaper by stripping the top layer down from the wall. The residue paper can be easily removed with a sponge and warm water.

Materials

Wallpaper is made from many different types of material. The following is a list and description of the various types of paper available, as well as possible uses and tips for hanging.

Vinyl Vinyl paper is the most popular and easiest to apply. It is relatively inexpensive and durable. Vinyl coverings are either backed with cloth or paper. Vinyl-coated paper has been sprayed with a thin coat of plastic. Both types are washable to varying degrees. Most come pretrimmed and prepasted. Vinyl is good to use in high traffic areas such as hallways, kitchens, and baths.

NOTE: Very thick heavy vinyls are very difficult to hang in small areas such as bathrooms where a lot of cutting and fitting is necessary.

Paper Paper wallpaper is just that, wallpaper made of plain paper with no coatings or special treatments. Paper usually requires paste and cannot be handled as much as vinyl because it rips and tears.

CAUTION: Do not overpaste or make the paper too soggy. This may cause water stains or the paper to turn pulpy while hanging.

Fiber cloths The most popular types of fiber cloths used in home decorating are grass cloth, burlap, hemp, and jute. The fibers are woven and laminated on a paper or cloth backing. The fibers contain natural irregularities so color, texture, and uniformity can vary. Due to these color and texture variations, the seams will show when the cloths are hung.

TIP: To hang fiber cloths so the seams will be less obvious, reverse every other strip. Hang the first strip top to bottom, cut the next strip, turn it around, and hang the bottom of the paper at the ceiling, the top at the floorboard.

Flock Flock is two-dimensional paper which resembles damask or cut velvet. This type of paper is usually used in formal rooms. Due to its texture, it is excellent for hiding imperfections on the walls. Flock can be tricky to hang because glue cannot be washed off easily on the front side and the material can easily become crushed while hanging.

HINT: To prevent damage to flock paper use a damp sponge, instead of a smoothing blade, to press into place on the wall.

Foils Foil wallpaper is made by laminating a thin metallic sheet to a paper or fabric backing. Many foils are coated with mylar which gives a mirror-like finish. The reflective qualities of foil can open up a space and brighten a room, or turn a drab room into a dazzling, modern one. Due to its finish and metallic properties, this paper does not "breathe," making air bubbles very hard to remove. Foils are also difficult to hang because they wrinkle easily, and show any imperfections on the wall's surface.

Murals Murals are used as "eye catchers," drawing the eye into a room, giving the illusion of a larger space. Murals usually depict a natural scenic setting. Some murals portray historical or symbolic settings of an event or era, while others are enlarged photos or copies of famous paintings. Murals are available on foil, paper, and vinyl, and need thorough surface preparation to look their best.

TIP: Hang murals over lining paper to ensure a smooth surface.

CHAPTER II
GETTING OFF TO THE RIGHT START

The Proper Tools Make All the Difference

As with any project, the "right tools for the right job" can mean the difference between a professional-looking effort and a disaster. While many stores carry wallpapering kits, it is better in the long run to buy quality tools separately.

Tools to Have

Scissors A good pair of stainless steel (prevents rust) sewing scissors are your best bet. Expensive (about $12 a pair) but worth it, especially if you plan to do several papering jobs.

One four- or six-foot level A level gives you a long consistent plumb line without the mess of a chalk plumb bob.

Two medium-size plastic buckets One for water, one for paste.

Two yardsticks One for measuring the paper, one for measuring the wall (saves running back and forth looking for your yardstick).

Square To make sure the paper is cut straight across. May help save paper when matching a tricky pattern.

Two pencils For marking cuts on paper and plumb line on wall.

Box of single-edge razor blades For cutting paper while hanging. Gives you greater control and accuracy than a matte knife.

Seam roller To smooth edges where two strips of paper meet. Also a tube of seam adhesive, although Elmer's glue will do in a pinch. Wooden rollers are better than plastic. Do not use seam roller on flock paper because it will damage edges. Use moist sponge to press down seams.

Hard plastic smoothing blade Smooths out paper easier than a brush. Do not get soft plastic (the razor will cut it to shreds while trimming), or metal (too hard, will cut paper to shreds).

Whisk For mixing glue. Gets out lumps better than a spoon.

Cutting and pasting table You do not want to cut and paste on your knees on the hard floor. A clean countertop is a good alternative.

Small pocket apron (nail aprons available at most hardware stores) Saves time wasted hunting for your tools.

Two sponges; one large, one small For smoothing and wetting paper (if prepasted).

Paste brush (natural bristles, not plastic) To apply glue to un-pasted paper.

Step ladder Either a four- or six-foot ladder (aluminum is lighter to move around). Using a shorter ladder allows you to stand on the ladder facing the wall. The paper is easier to hang when you are closer to the wall without having to reach over the top of a tall ladder.

Hands Your hands are you best tools. They are used in every step of the paperhanging process. Take care of them. Remove rings. Keep nails clipped and wash glue off when finished hanging each strip. Avoid chapping.

Tools to Avoid

Plumb bob An exact plumb line is essential for hanging paper straight. A plumb bob is not as accurate as a level, and can be very messy. Also, the chalk line will show through lighter paper.

Pasting tray Used for wetting down prepasted paper. Not very practical. The paper sticks together and is hard to wet down in such a narrow container. Not enough control over how much water is applied.

Roller Rollers (usually paint rollers) used for smoothing paper do not give you the hardness, pressure, or control needed to get out all the air bubbles. You should only use a paint roller and tray for applying sizing.

Trim wheel This gadget is intended to perforate the paper so you can tear it off at the proper place while trimming around windows and floorboards. You always seem to tear the paper instead, as the wheel never seems to cut well.

Smoothing brush Can be useful if the bristles are short and firm. Not as efficient or effective as a hard plastic smoothing blade. However, the brush is better than the blade for use on flock paper because it causes less abrasion.

Matte knife A hand-held single-edged razor blade offers more control in cutting.

How to Measure and Buy

Most paper is sold in double rolls. However, wallpaper is priced by the single roll. A double roll covers roughly 72 square feet or 54 square feet depending on the width. Some papers are also available in triple rolls. Widths vary, but the most common are 20 1/2 inches or 27 inches.

Measuring Your Room

To determine how much paper to buy, measure the room to find the total square footage. With this number, a sales clerk should be able to tell you how many rolls you will need of your particular selection. Or you can determine how much paper you will need by dividing the square footage a double roll covers into the total square footage of your room. This will give you the number of double rolls needed to cover your walls.

To measure a room for surface area:
- Measure the height and width (in feet) of each wall.
- Multiply width by height to get the area of each wall in square footage.
- Add together surface areas of all the walls.
- Subtract from that total the square footage area of any doors and windows. This will give you the total wall area to be covered.

This is the square footage measurement to take to the store when you buy your paper. Always round up fractions. If in doubt, buy that extra roll. Unopened rolls can be returned.

Buying Your Paper

Wallpaper is priced by the single roll but sold by the double or triple roll. The paper books or labels on rolls of in-stock paper will tell you how many square feet a double roll will cover. Divide the total square footage of wall surface area by the square footage of a double roll of the paper you want to buy. This will give you the number of double rolls needed to paper your room.

Allow for pattern repeats, especially in a drop match pattern.

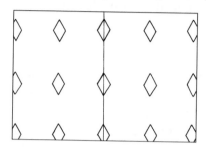

straight match

drop match

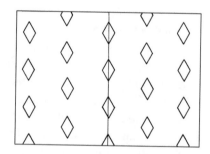

Drop match paper has more waste and usually requires more paper than a straight across match. The repeat spacing can be found in the pattern books. To make allowances for a large repeat, compute this simple formula:

- Measure height of wall.
- Divide height by number of inches between pattern repeat.
- Round up.
- Multiply this number by pattern repeat number.

This is the actual wall height measurement you must use when computing the square footage of the room you want to paper.

Example:

- wall height 85 inches
- pattern repeat 12 inches
- 85 divided by 12 equals 7.1

- rounded up is 8
- 8 x 12 = 96
- 96 inches must be used as the wall height in calculating the square footage of the room

In the above example, the pattern repeat makes a great difference in how much wallpaper must be ordered.

RULE OF THUMB: **If in doubt, always order the extra roll**

CHAPTER III
PREPARING THE WALLS

One of the secrets to a professional-looking job is a well-prepared surface. Take time to do a thorough preparation. For the best wallpapering results, a clean wall free of any imperfections is the ideal. However, sometimes this is not possible (especially in old houses) without replastering the wall. Wallpaper, depending on the thickness and pattern, can cover up many wall imperfections. Liner paper can also be used. In general, try to make the surface as smooth and clean as possible.

An important part of the prepping process involves removing any fixtures (switch plates, light fixtures, small cabinets, curtain rods, etc.) from the room, as well as the furniture if possible. The more space you have to move around in, the better.

Removing Old Paper

If the existing wallpaper is only one layer thick and in good condition, you can probably paper over it with little difficulty. However, if you are papering with a non-porous paper, such as foil, remove all old paper to prevent mildew.

Papering over old wallpaper is always risky as the moisture in the adhesive can loosen the old paper or get trapped between the layers and cause mildew. To be on the safe side take off old paper unless it is very tight on the walls. Even then old paper may buckle under newly applied wet paper.

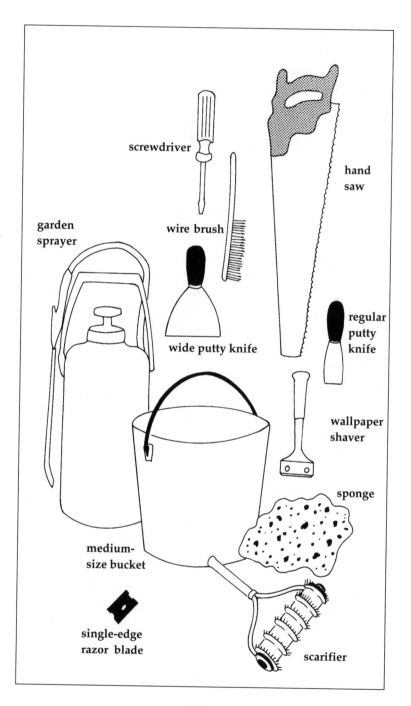

screwdriver

hand saw

garden sprayer

wire brush

wide putty knife

regular putty knife

wallpaper shaver

sponge

medium-size bucket

single-edge razor blade

scarifier

When not to remove

Unsealed wallboard Drywall which has not been sealed by a thick coat of paint before papering is almost impossible to remove paper from without extensive damage to the walls. If the wallboard tears off with the paper, leave the paper on, seal it with a primer, and use joint compound to fill in or smooth over rough spots.

Canvas covering Canvas was used to preserve plaster walls by covering over cracks and keeping walls smooth. If at all possible leave this covering on the plaster, patch any rough spots, size it, and paper over it. If you must take the canvas off due to its poor condition, it is hard to avoid taking off the finish coat of plaster as well. Be prepared to replaster or patch the walls.

Tools for Prepping Your Walls

The tools you will need to remove old paper will depend on the type of paper on the wall. Some of the tools useful for removing wallpaper are:

Liquid chemical remover Chemical remover available at the hardware store is dissolved in hot water and sprayed or sponged on old wallpaper to break down the adhesive making the paper easier to remove.

Wallpaper scraper or shaver Designed specifically for wallpaper removal. Comes with replaceable blades. The blade is thick, small, and angled for more efficient paper removal.

Putty/broad knife One putty and one broad knife are useful for dry scrapes or on more delicate walls such as drywall where it is easy to damage with vigorous scraping.

Screwdriver Used for removal of fixtures before papering.

Single-edge razor blade For scoring paper to allow chemical remover to soak through the paper for easier removal. Other tools used for scoring are hand saw, scarifier, wire brush.

Disposable plastic drop cloth To protect your floor and furniture from the water.

   HINT: Tape drop cloth to floorboard to hold in place.

Large plastic garbage bags To deposit paper once removed from walls.

Large sponge and bucket Use to apply liquid remover.

Rubber gloves To protect hands from chemical remover.
Garden sprayer For applying chemical remover to walls.

Techniques for Removing Wallpaper

First determine what type of paper is on the walls. Depending on the type, the paper can be removed in one of four ways: dry scrape, peelable/strippable, liquid chemical remover, or steamer.

TIP: **Start removing the paper the easiest way (pulling it off the wall) and work up to the more difficult (steamer) to see what it takes to remove the paper.**

Strippable/Peelable Paper

Take the putty knife to the corner or seam of the paper to pry up an edge. Pull the wallcovering up. If it pulls away from the wall in one piece easily it is strippable. If it pulls away from the wall leaving a thin layer of paper backing it is peelable. You can sometimes use this backing as a liner for the new wallpaper or it can be easily removed with warm water and a scraper. If the paper starts to tear and comes off in tiny strips, it is non-strippable and must be removed by another method.

Dry Scrape

Old wallpaper may be dry enough to scrape off with a putty or broad knife. Run your fingers over the paper. If it crackles or has large air bubbles, break into the paper with a putty knife and scrape off the paper. This method will work best if the paper is dry and brittle and the walls are plaster. After you have dry scraped off all the paper, you can wet down the remaining pieces and remove with a wallpaper scraper.

Wet Scrape

Liquid chemical remover can be applied using a garden sprayer or large sponge and bucket of water. A garden sprayer containing chemical remover and hot water is best if you have a large surface area to cover. This method is messier and the possibility of water damage to floor and furniture is greater. With a sponge and bucket of chemical remover, your wall coverage is slower but you have more control over the amount of remover you

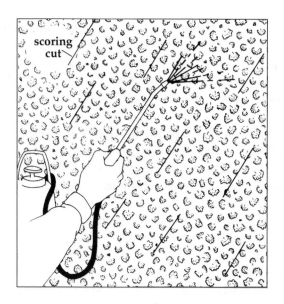

put on the wall and can soak an area more thoroughly with little mess. Either way you should score or scrape the walls first with a razor, saw, or other tool to allow the remover to break down the old adhesive. After spraying or sponging, wait 5 to 10 minutes for the chemical to soften the wallpaper. Mop up any excess water. When the paper bubbles up you can scrape it off with a broad knife or paper scraper. If the paper dries out, reapply the remover. If you start to scrape too soon, you will damage your wall and work harder than necessary.

HINT: **Be careful when scraping a paper which has been applied over wallboard. Wallboard is quickly damaged by vigorous scraping.**

Fiber wallcovering removal requires a two-step process. The fibers are glued to a backing so you must wet and remove the fibers first and then the paper backing.

TIP: **If you plan to paint the walls after paper removal, be sure to clean all adhesive off before painting to prevent cracks in the paint.**

Steamer

Steamers can be rented from paper and paint stores. If you can avoid using a steamer, do so. The hot water and steam can be dangerous, it is cumbersome to work with, and only steams off a small area of paper at a time. But, because a steamer penetrates more deeply with fewer applications than a chemical remover, it may be more desirable for certain jobs. A steamer is best used to remove multi-layers of old paper wallpaper.

Preparing Walls for Long-Lasting Adhesion

Wallpaper can conceal many imperfections in your walls, but it is best to start with a smooth clean surface. Thin or light-colored papers, and foils will show imperfections more readily than thicker multi-patterned vinyls.

The first step in papering your room is to remove any and all fixtures, shelves, etc., from the walls.

Plaster and Patch

Use joint compound to fill holes and smooth over imperfections. If you have plaster walls, you may have to use plaster to repair major damage where you can see the lath. To repair drywall, let damaged area dry thoroughly after removing old paper, cut away any tears in drywall with a razor blade, then spackle any depression or holes.

Prime or Line

On drywall, you may have to paint the walls with a flat oil-based paint so moisture is not absorbed into the wall when papering. This also allows you to remove the new paper easily at a later date.

HINT: If walls are shiny and slick, rough them up with medium grain sandpaper or the wallpaper will not adhere properly.

If your walls are in rough condition or you cannot remove a heavy layer of paper, lining your walls with give you a smooth surface on which to paper. This is especially true of old houses. Liner paper also works well over paneling (which is extremely difficult to remove) before you paper.

HINT: Be sure to size the liner paper with a special heavy duty premixed sizing before you paper. Liner paper is very porous and will absorb the adhesive of the wallpaper causing the paper to come off unless the liner is sized first.

Sizing the Walls

Sizing the walls is a very important step in your wallpaper project. Sizing helps wallpaper to adhere better to the walls and makes the paper easier to remove should you decide on a new paper at a later date. Premixed sizing is available for very porous walls or liner paper. However, powdered sizing mixed with water is most often used and will work for most papering jobs. After mixing, pour your sizing into a paint tray and apply with a roller and brush as you would paint. Go slow. Sizing is thin and will splatter.

Preparing Various Wall Surfaces

Newly plastered walls Make sure the walls are thoroughly dry and cured before you paper. Seal walls with a coat of flat oil-based primer sealer. Size walls, then hang wallpaper.

New wallboard If not already done, tape and seal all joints between panels of wallboard. Let dry, then sand walls smooth and apply a coat of flat oil-based primer sealer. When primer has dried, size wall and hang paper.

Painted walls Wash off dirt, oil, and grease and let dry. If paint is high gloss, rough up walls with sandpaper and size before you paper. If paint is a dark color, apply one coat of flat oil-based primer over it to prevent color from showing through wallpaper.

Textured walls Textured walls such as rough plaster, wood, or concrete require thorough cleaning and at least one undercoat of sealer before you can paper. Many of these surfaces also need to be covered with a heavy liner paper first. Don't forget to size the liner paper before hanging your wallpaper. Use a heavy grade premixed paste for hanging the liner paper.

Mildewed walls Mildew must be removed from walls along with any mildewed wallpaper before you hang the new wallpaper. Scrub mildewed wall with a hard bristle brush using a prepared concentrated liquid available from the paint store or a mixture of one cup trisodium phosphate, 1/2 cup strong detergent (liquid), one quart of bleach, and one gallon of water. After removing mildew, let the wall dry for at least 24 hours. Apply one thick coat of oil-based primer sealer and let dry.

<u>HINT:</u> Add a small amount of fungicide additive to the sealer to ensure a mildew-free surface. Size walls and hang paper.

Painting Woodwork and Ceiling
The last step before you paper a room is to paint the woodwork and ceiling. Now you are ready to begin hanging your paper!

CHAPTER IV
HANGING YOUR WALLPAPER

Inspect the Paper
Inspect the rolls of wallpaper for imperfections (inconsistent color, fading, blotches, rips). Unroll the paper. Do not cut any paper before you inspect the entire roll. If imperfections are found, return the entire roll to the store. Make sure you find the same run number on all rolls. If rolls of paper were printed on different runs, the colors might not match exactly. If all is well, you can begin to hang the paper.

Find a Starting Place
Pick an inconspicuous place to hang your first strip. As you move around the room from left to right, chances are the last strip you hang will not match up to the first strip, so you want that match to be as inconspicuous as possible. Start your first strip on a corner, an alcove, or to one side of a door or window. If there is a natural break in the room such as a floor-to-ceiling closet, start on one side of it and finish on the other.

Hang Your Paper Straight
It is essential that wallpaper be hung straight. Unfortunately, most walls and corners are never "true" — vertical, perpendicular, or square. To compensate, you must align your first piece of paper (and every initial piece after you turn each corner) with a "true" vertical line called a plumb line.

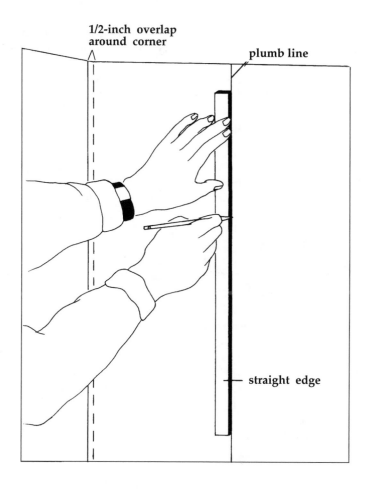

1/2-inch overlap around corner

plumb line

straight edge

Measure the width of your paper. Use your level to draw a "true" vertical line 1/2 inch less than the width of the paper from your starting point in the room. For example, the paper is 20 1/2 inches wide. You choose to start at one corner of the room. Take your yardstick, measure out 20 inches from the corner, and make a mark on the wall. Place the level vertically against that mark (aligning the bubbles between the marks on the level to ensure a straight vertical line) and draw a straight line down the wall using your level as a guide. Because you left a half inch of space, the paper will overlap the corner, which will help compensate if the corner is not square.

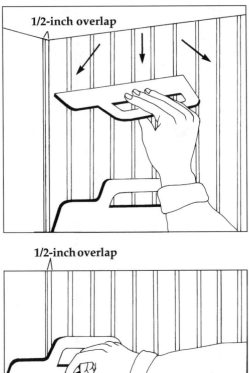

Cutting the Paper

Measuring for Length

Measure and cut a strip the length of your wall plus 4 inches (2 inches at the top and 2 inches at the bottom) for trimming. Use a square to make a clean cut evenly across the paper. When measuring out the paper, be sure to make only small pencil marks which will not show once the paper is hung.

> HINT: Cut full strips of paper. Do not try to cut out a portion of paper which will overlap doors and windows. Cut around opening while hanging the full strip of paper on the wall.

Taking Pattern into Account

Unroll the paper and look at the pattern to determine a good marker. A marker can be a flower, color, or design on the right side of the paper, so when the next strip is put up to the right of the first one, it will be easy to match. Cut 2 inches above the marker so that when you hang the paper with the marker at the top, you will have an overlap to trim in case of an uneven ceiling line (most ceilings are not square). Make sure the left side of the second strip matches the correct marker on the right side of the first strip.

TIP: A good way to stretch your paper and save waste is to alternate rolls when cutting each strip.

Pasting

Using ready-to-mix powder Powdered paste, ready to mix, comes in several types. Wheat paste for use on regular paper; vinyl paste for use on vinyl and vinyl-coated paper; and cellulose paste for use on foils or heavy vinyls. To mix, pour the amount of water (see package instructions) needed into a bucket. Slowly pour paste into water stirring with a whisk to eliminate lumps. When the mixture is smooth and has the consistency of runny glue, let stand for 10 minutes. The paste will thicken some and might need to be thinned with water before applying to paper. When mixed correctly, the paste should not run off the paper when hanging or gel into large lumps. If you don't want to use a whole package of paste, pour out the amount of water into a bucket you will need and then slowly add small amounts of paste until the mixture is the proper consistency to use.

Using premixed paste Premixed paste comes in various strengths and types and will not mildew non-porous (heavy vinyl or foil) paper. Premixed paste also holds paper to the wall longer and tighter, but can stain the front of the paper if not wiped immediately.

Application

Non-pasted paper Lay the first strip face down on the pasting table. Mix paste per instructions with a whisk. Start at the top third of the paper, brushing a coat of paste on evenly until the paper is completely covered. Do not miss any small areas or you will have "blisters" (unpasted spots in your finished paper). Gently fold the pasted area over on itself, but don't crease the paper at the fold. Paste the next two thirds and fold the paper up so it resembles an accordion fold.

HINT: **Let the paper cure (sit) a few minutes before hanging.**

Prepasted paper Use a bucket of water and a large sponge. Squeeze sponge gently over the paper. Then rub the water around on the paper in circular motions until the entire area you are wetting has a thin layer of paste on it. Do not make the paper too wet and soggy. You can always add more water as needed. Paste the paper using water the same way as unpasted paper in an accordion fold.

TIP: **Prepasted paper should never be dunked in water. This might cause the paper to become too wet and pasty, making it extremely difficult to work with.**

Special Considerations — Bathrooms and Kitchens

Due to the moisture content of kitchens and bathrooms, wallpaper will adhere longer and better in these two rooms if you use a premixed paste even if the paper you want to hang is already prepasted. Light vinyl-coated papers are best for these rooms.

Hanging Wallpaper

Carry the accordion folded strip of paper to the wall, mount the ladder, unfold the top third, and press the upper side edge along the vertical level line you drew on the wall. Smooth lightly with your hand so the piece stays on while you continue dropping the paper down, aligning the right side against the plumb line. Starting from the top, smooth down the center of the paper and from the center out to the sides as you move down the strip of paper to the floorboard.

Before the paste dries, the paper will have some "give" for you to gently slide it around to line it up correctly, matching the left side to the right side of the strip preceding it.

When the paper is smooth against the wall and all air bubbles and extra paste have been smoothed or brushed out, use the one-sided razor blade to cut off the excess strip at the top and bottom.

<u>TIP:</u> **As a straight edge guide for cutting, use the smoothing blade along the ceiling and floorboard between the paper and razor.**

Each subsequent strip is hung in exactly the same manner, with the pattern carefully matched if applicable.

Types of Seams

Butt seam The seam used most often is the butt seam. This seam is the easiest to do and the least noticeable. Butt the edge of the strip of paper you are hanging to the one previously hung. Do not stretch the wallpaper.

> <u>TIP:</u> **Make sure you cure the paper so it won't shrink or bubble up on the wall causing the seam to come apart.**

Lap seam Today, the lap seam is almost never used except on inside corners. The edge of one strip is hung 1/2 inch or less over the previously hung strip. (See Chapter V)

> <u>HINT:</u> **Overlap away from the entry to the room. The seam will be less noticeable.**

Double cut seam When there is an irregularity in the wall or a mistake in drawing the plumb line, one edge of the strip you are hanging will unevenly overlap the edge of the previously hung strip. Keep the overlap, and then place the smoothing blade or straight edge at the center of the overlap and cut through both layers of wallpaper using the razor blade. Remove the top overlap section. Peel back edge of top strip and remove the bottom cut-off section. Smooth both seams down and they should butt tightly together.

> <u>TIP:</u> **This type of seam usually causes a pattern mismatch so you may find it less conspicuous it you just leave the overlap.**

Common Problems and Mistakes

Misalignment Wallpaper wrinkles and does not butt properly to previously hung strip.

> Cure: Lift off strip and realign.

Air bubbles Smooth out bubbles as you hang strip of paper. Small bubbles will usually disappear when dry.

> Cure: Large persistent bubbles — take off strip and let cure or release trapped air with razor and smooth out.

Loose edges or seams which curl or pull loose.

>Cure: Lift edge gently and reapply paste with a small brush or your fingertips. If edges still do not stay down, try seam glue or Elmer's glue.

Damaged areas or large tears Place larger piece of wallpaper over the damaged area until the pattern matches. Tack corners of patch on wall. Using a straight edge, cut a square around the damaged section through the two layers of paper. Remove tacks and lift out the patch and the damaged section. Clean wall area under damaged paper. Paste the patch and position it against the wall. Smooth into place matching it to the other paper.

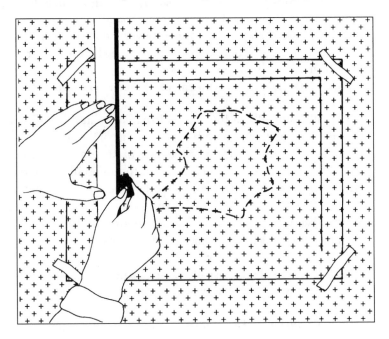

Paper cut too short If you accidentally cut a strip too short and don't want to cut another strip due to waste, align and smooth the short piece into place on the wall, match and cut a strip of paper from your scraps to finish out the short piece plus 2 inches. Place small strip just under larger strip matching across horizontally. Smoothing down the top strip, make sure it matches across the small scrap piece. Trim as usual along the baseboard.

CHAPTER V
SPECIAL TECHNIQUES

Hanging Around Openings

Outlets

Smooth the wallpaper over the opening. Carefully cut an X into the paper right up to the corners of the opening with a sharp razor. Cut off loose flaps with the scissors.

Immovable Objects

If you come to an object such as a thermostat which cannot be removed, smooth the paper up to the edge of the fixture. Cut an X over the fixture and gradually make the opening larger until the paper can be smoothed around the perimeter of the fixture. Trim off excess with the razor.

Doors and Windows

When a strip of paper overhangs a door or window opening, smooth the paper as close to the edge as possible without buckling

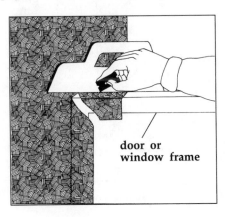

door or
window frame

the paper. Cut a 45-degree diagonal to the corners of the opening and use the edge of the smoothing blade to tap paper into the corner where the wall meets the window or door frame. Trim excess with a razor and straight edge of your smoothing blade.

Curved Archways

Hang the wallpaper above and around the arch letting the excess paper hang freely. Cut the paper so it overlaps the arch by one inch on the inside edge of the arch. Then make small wedge-shaped cuts in the paper up to the edge of the arch around the entire arch. Wrap the cut edges to the inside of the arch. It is OK for edges to overlap. Then cut a strip the width of the underside of the arch minus 1/8 inch to prevent catching and fraying.

Hanging Around Corners

Inside Corners

When you get to less than a full strip's width from the corner, measure the distance from the edge of the previous strip to the corner in at least three places. Take the largest of these measure-

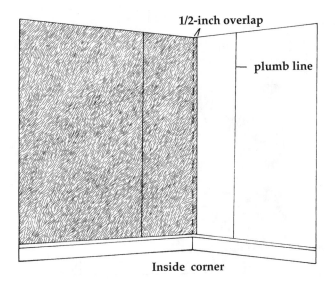

Inside corner

ments, add one inch overlap to get around the corner, and cut the strip vertically to this width.

Hang the partial strip, butting it against the previous strip and lapping it around the corner. Use sponge to push paper gently into the corner.

Measure the width of the remaining part of the strip. Then measure that same distance out from the corner on the new wall and draw a vertical line with your level.

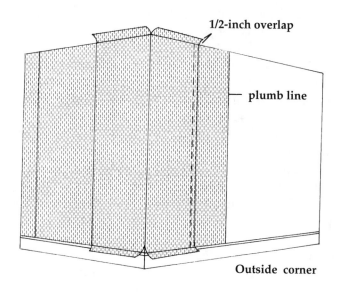

1/2-inch overlap

plumb line

Outside corner

Hang the remainder of the divided strip, aligning it carefully along the new plumb line. The two parts of the original whole strip are now overlapped about an inch.

Outside Corners

The problem with outside corners is similar to inside corners: the two walls are not likely to be plumb and the corner is not likely to be square. The strip that turns the corner will be split with a one-inch overlap, and the part that goes on the new wall is hung to a new vertical plumb line. However, since a seam on an outside corner is more conspicuous than on an inside corner, you should first try going around the corner with the paper intact. If the walls are fairly plumb, you can fudge a bit by lining up the second strip on the new wall on a plumb line and having it overlap the corner strip by 1/4 of an inch.

Ceilings

Papering a ceiling can be cumbersome. If you are not experienced in wallpaper hanging, the best alternative is to paint the ceiling. However, if you choose to paper your ceiling, a few good tips will make the job easier.

- Paper the ceiling before the walls to avoid spoiling other work.
- Use a random-patterned coordinate paper with easy matches or none (such as a stripe) to make the job easier.
- Paper across the shortest distance of the ceiling to avoid long awkward strips.
- Paper with a helper. It is almost impossible to paper a ceiling without another pair of arms to hold the remaining length up while you align it along the plumb line and smooth the paper down.

Hanging paper on the ceiling

Papering a ceiling is the same as hanging paper on a wall except you are working overhead, standing on a scaffold. Prep the ceiling as you would the wall. To mark off the first plumb line measure 1/2 inch less than the width of the paper because you want a 1/2-inch overhang on the wall. This avoids gaps between ceiling and wallpaper where the ceiling meets the wall. Again, you want to cut each strip of paper four inches longer than needed so it will overlap onto the walls two inches at each end.

Mark the plumb lines as you go. You might want to use a chalk line in this case because it is easier to snap a chalk line than to hold a level upside down and draw a pencil line along it. However, you will need a yardstick to make sure the line is plumb. Making adjustments while papering due to poor plumb lines on the ceiling is very difficult.

Apply paste and fold paper accordion style. Line up strip with plumb line and smooth down first section along the plumb line, gently pushing the paper into the corner and edges of the ceiling. Have the other person hold the remaining folds of paper up with a broom while you work your way across the ceiling to the other side.

Slanted Wall or Dormer

Slanted walls (usually found in finished attics or second-story dormers) require a few different techniques than straight walls. Like a ceiling, it is best to use a simple multi-directional pattern. Stripes are not recommended because the slant of the upper wall can throw off the alignment.

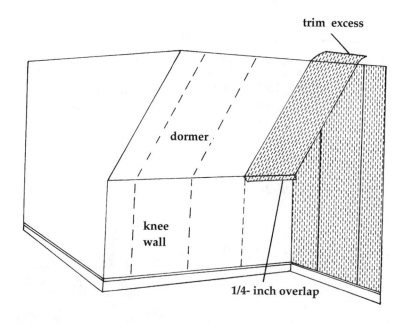

Finish papering the wall adjacent to the slanted wall leaving 1/2 inch overlap on the slanted wall. Using a level for your plumb line, paper across the slanted portion first, leaving a 1/2-inch overlap on the knee wall. Continue the plumb line down the knee wall from the slanted portion and paper across the knee wall matching the top of the paper to upper slanted portion overlapping the knee wall paper on the overhang. Where the knee wall and the slanted wall meet will not be perfectly square so you will probably have to make some adjustments.

Stairwells

Again, you will find the papering job easier if you have a helper to hold the remaining folds of the wet paper which can become quite heavy when hanging one long strip down the stairwell wall.

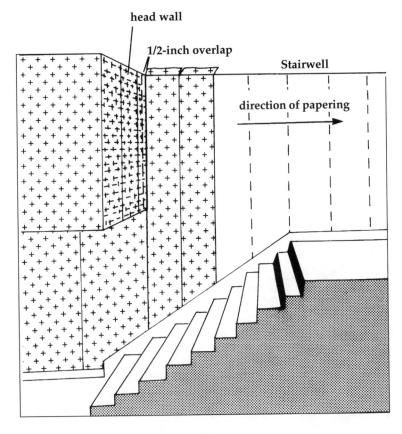

Measure the longest vertical distance from ceiling to baseboard. Paper going up the stairs, hanging the longest strip first. This way, you hang one full strip, without cuts and adjustments, around the head wall. Using a level, mark a vertical plumb line 1/2 inch less than the width of the paper. Cut and paste the paper as usual (don't forget to add the 2-inch overhang at the top and bottom of the paper when measuring) Standing on the scaffold, hang the first strip along the plumb line to your right with 1/2 inch overlap on the head wall (if you have one) to your left. Smooth paper down and trim top and bottom.

> HINT: If you are sure the paper is properly aligned along the plumb line, trim the top of the paper before you smooth the rest of the paper down. This will reduce the number of times you get on and off the scaffold. Or, have a helper smooth down bottom portion and cut and paste the next strip so you can stay on the scaffold.

On the head wall, start with a full strip on the outside corner edge working left to right toward the inside corner where your first stairwell strip has been overlapped.

FINAL WORDS

Remember to have fun! Think of wallpapering as putting together a beautiful jigsaw puzzle on your wall. All the pieces should fit perfectly if you are patient, and the change in your room decor will be dramatic!

NOTES